HAL•LEONARD

Jazz Play Along®

Book and CD for B♭, E♭, C and Bass Clef Instruments

volume **74**

Produced by Mark Taylor

Arranged by
Mark Taylor and Jim Roberts

Best of Jazz CLASSICS

10 FAVORITE TUNES

BOOK

CD

ISBN-13: 978-1-4234-2617-2
ISBN-10: 1-4234-2617-7

HAL•LEONARD®
CORPORATION

7777 W. BLUEMOUND RD. P.O. BOX 13819 MILWAUKEE, WI 53213

Visit Hal Leonard Online at
www.halleonard.com

Best Jazz Classics

Volume 74

Produced by Mark Taylor
Arranged by Mark Taylor and Jim Roberts

Featured Players:

Graham Breedlove–Trumpet
John Desalme–Saxophones
Tony Nalker–Piano
Jim Roberts–Bass

HOW TO USE THE CD:

Each song has <u>two</u> tracks:

1) Split Track/Melody

Woodwind, Brass, Keyboard, and **Mallet Players** can use this track as a learning tool for melody style and inflection.

Bass Players can learn and perform with this track – remove the recorded bass track by turning down the volume on the LEFT channel.

Keyboard and **Guitar Players** can learn and perform with this track – remove the recorded piano part by turning down the volume on the RIGHT channel.

2) Full Stereo Track

Soloists or **Groups** can learn and perform with this accompaniment track with the RHYTHM SECTION only.

ALL TOO SOON

WORDS AND MUSIC BY DUKE ELLINGTON
AND CARL SIGMAN

CD

◆3 : SPLIT TRACK/MELODY
◆4 : FULL STEREO TRACK

C VERSION

AZURE-TE
(PARIS BLUES)

WRITTEN BY BILL DAVID
AND DON WOLF

CHERYL

CD
5 : SPLIT TRACK/MELODY
6 : FULL STEREO TRACK

C VERSION

BY CHARLIE PARKER

SOLOS (10 CHORUSES)

D.S. AL FINE

GINGER BREAD BOY

BY JIMMY HEATH

C VERSION

DON'T EXPLAIN

WORDS AND MUSIC BY BILLIE HOLIDAY
AND ARTHUR HERZOG

CD

◆**7** : SPLIT TRACK/MELODY

◆**8** : FULL STEREO TRACK

C VERSION

JORDU

BY DUKE JORDAN

CD

11: SPLIT TRACK/MELODY

12: FULL STEREO TRACK

C VERSION

JUMP FOR JOY

BY DUKE ELLINGTON,
PAUL WEBSTER AND SID KULLER

C VERSION

TWO BASS HIT

CD
- ◆15 : SPLIT TRACK/MELODY
- ◆16 : FULL STEREO TRACK

BY DIZZY GILLESPIE
AND JOHN LEWIS

C VERSION FAST SWING

UP JUMPED SPRING

BY FREDDIE HUBBARD

C VERSION

19

CD
◆19◆ : SPLIT TRACK/MELODY
◆20◆ : FULL STEREO TRACK

YOU CALL IT MADNESS
(BUT I CALL IT LOVE)

WORDS AND MUSIC BY CON CONRAD, GLADYS DUBOIS,
RUSS COLUMBO AND PAUL GREGORY

C VERSION

CHERYL

By Charlie Parker

Bb Version

ALL TOO SOON

WORDS AND MUSIC BY DUKE ELLINGTON
AND CARL SIGMAN

Bb VERSION   MEDIUM SWING

CD

AZURE-TE
(PARIS BLUES)

WRITTEN BY BILL DAVID
AND DON WOLF

Bb VERSION

MOD. SWING

DON'T EXPLAIN

WORDS AND MUSIC BY BILLIE HOLIDAY
AND ARTHUR HERZOG

Bb VERSION

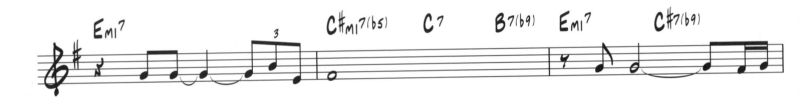

27

GINGER BREAD BOY

BY JIMMY HEATH

B♭ VERSION

CD

11 : SPLIT TRACK/MELODY
12 : FULL STEREO TRACK

JORDU

BY DUKE JORDAN

Bb VERSION

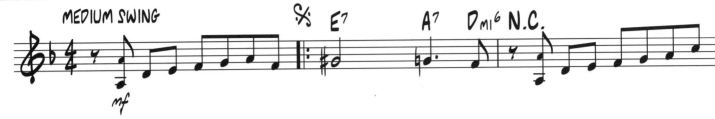

Jump for Joy

BY DUKE ELLINGTON,
PAUL WEBSTER AND SID KULLER

TWO BASS HIT

BY DIZZY GILLESPIE
AND JOHN LEWIS

CD
- **15**: SPLIT TRACK/MELODY
- **16**: FULL STEREO TRACK

B♭ VERSION   FAST SWING

UP JUMPED SPRING

BY FREDDIE HUBBARD

Bb VERSION

37

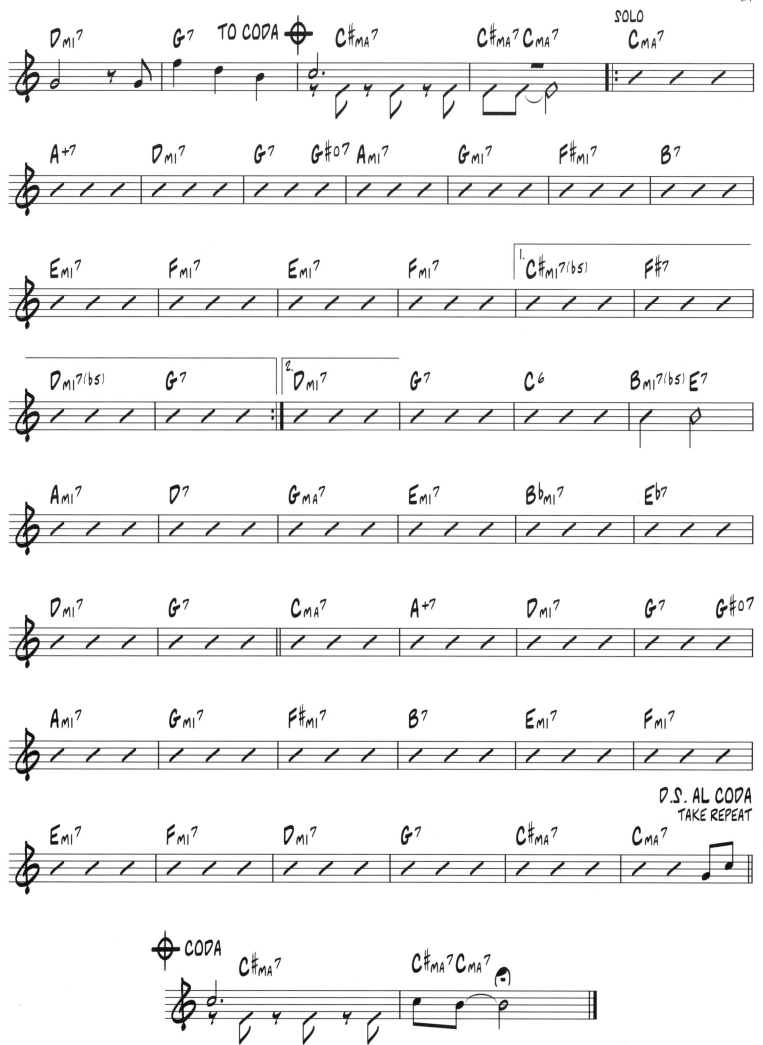

ALL TOO SOON

WORDS AND MUSIC BY DUKE ELLINGTON
AND CARL SIGMAN

E♭ VERSION

CD
❸ : SPLIT TRACK/MELODY
❹ : FULL STEREO TRACK

AZURE-TE
(PARIS BLUES)

WRITTEN BY BILL DAVID
AND DON WOLF

E♭ VERSION

MOD. SWING

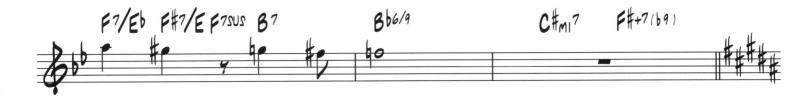

CHERYL

BY CHARLIE PARKER

CD

◆5 : SPLIT TRACK/MELODY
◆6 : FULL STEREO TRACK

E♭ VERSION

GINGER BREAD BOY

BY JIMMY HEATH

DON'T EXPLAIN

CD

◆ 7 : SPLIT TRACK/MELODY
◆ 8 : FULL STEREO TRACK

WORDS AND MUSIC BY BILLIE HOLIDAY
AND ARTHUR HERZOG

E♭ VERSION

SWING BALLAD

45

CD
11 : SPLIT TRACK/MELODY
12 : FULL STEREO TRACK

JORDU

BY DUKE JORDAN

E♭ VERSION

JUMP FOR JOY

BY DUKE ELLINGTON,
PAUL WEBSTER AND SID KULLER

Eb VERSION

TWO BASS HIT

CD
⬥15 : SPLIT TRACK/MELODY
⬥16 : FULL STEREO TRACK

BY DIZZY GILLESPIE
AND JOHN LEWIS

E♭ VERSION

FAST SWING

UP JUMPED SPRING

BY FREDDIE HUBBARD

53

CHERYL

BY CHARLIE PARKER

𝄢: C VERSION

ALL TOO SOON

WORDS AND MUSIC BY DUKE ELLINGTON
AND CARL SIGMAN

AZURE-TE
(PARIS BLUES)

WRITTEN BY BILL DAVID
AND DON WOLF

DON'T EXPLAIN

WORDS AND MUSIC BY BILLIE HOLIDAY
AND ARTHUR HERZOG

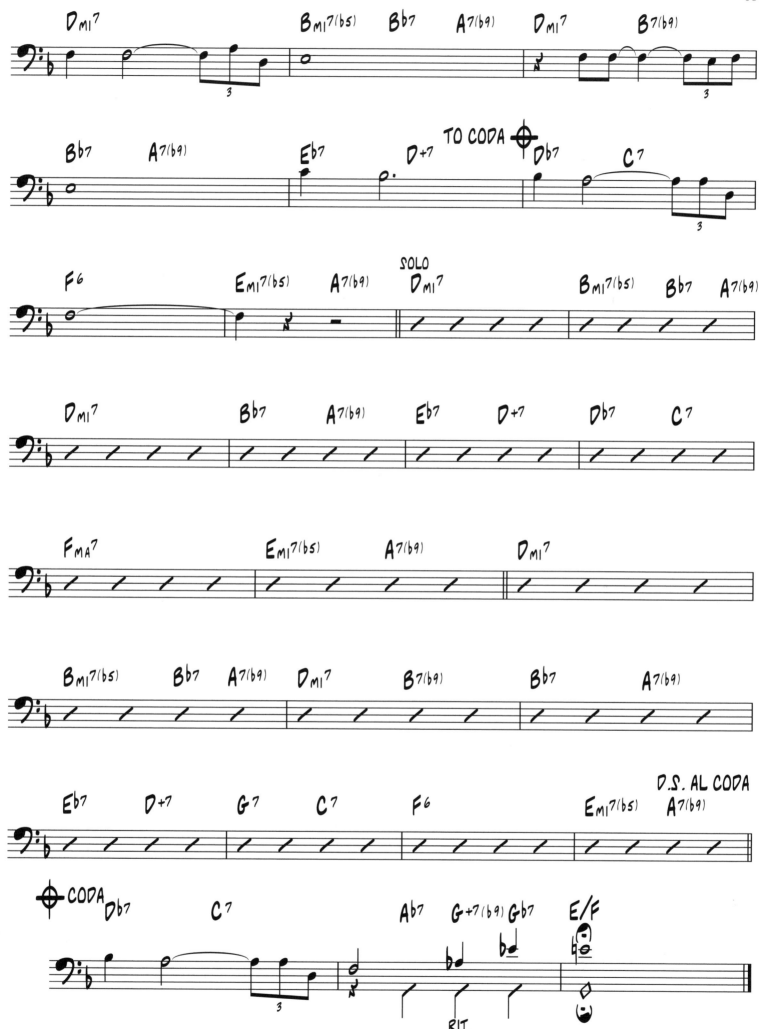

CD
- ◆ 9 : SPLIT TRACK/MELODY
- ◆ 10 : FULL STEREO TRACK

GINGER BREAD BOY

BY JIMMY HEATH

𝄢: C VERSION

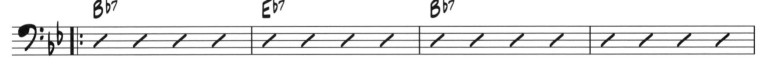

YOU CALL IT MADNESS
(BUT I CALL IT LOVE)

WORDS AND MUSIC BY CON CONRAD, GLADYS DUBOIS,
RUSS COLUMBO AND PAUL GREGORY

JORDU

BY DUKE JORDAN

JUMP FOR JOY

BY DUKE ELLINGTON,
PAUL WEBSTER AND SID KULLER

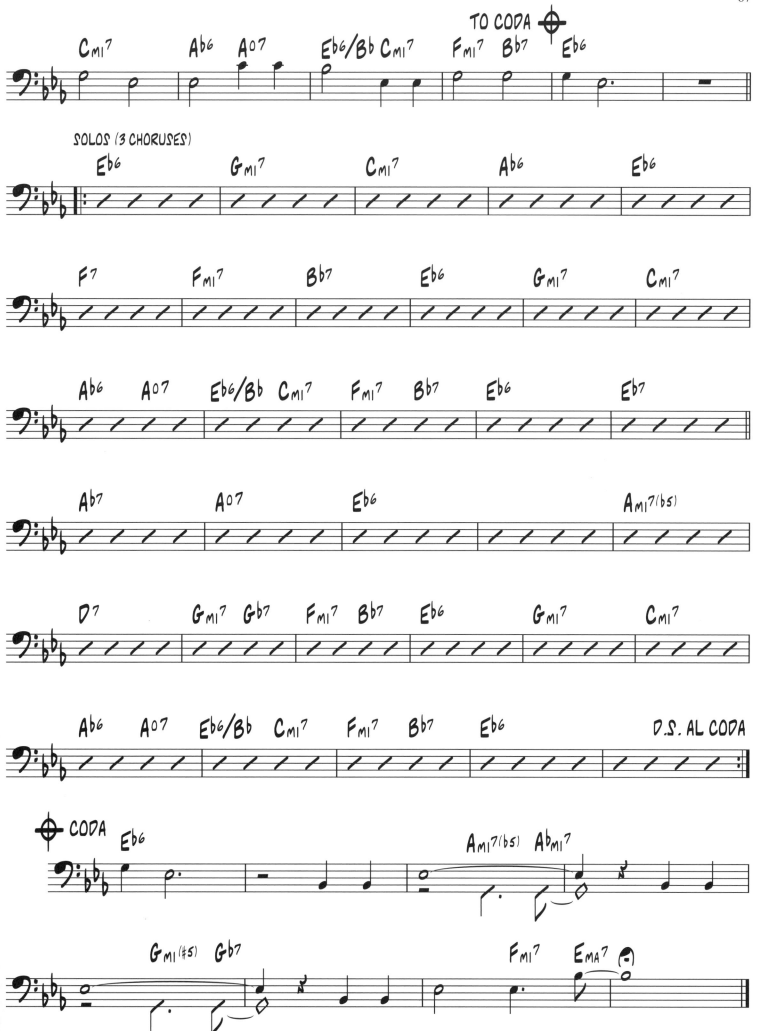

CD

TWO BASS HIT

BY DIZZY GILLESPIE
AND JOHN LEWIS

C VERSION

FAST SWING

UP JUMPED SPRING

BY FREDDIE HUBBARD

CD
- 17 : SPLIT TRACK/MELODY
- 18 : FULL STEREO TRACK

𝄢 : C VERSION

71